peace

A Highly Favoured Life Devotional

Copyright © The Highly Favoured Life 2024

Published and Designed by Unmovable Publications

ALL RIGHTS RESERVED to The Highly Favoured Life and authorized writers.

No part of this book may be reproduced, transmitted, or sold in any form or by any means, electronic, or mechanical, including photocopying, recording, or by any information storage and retrieval system, without permission in writing from the publisher.

All scripture quotations are from the King James Version (KJV) of the Bible.

1st Edition published in 2024
2nd Edition published in 2025

ISBN:
978-1-967189-12-0 (paperback)
978-1-967189-13-7 (hardback

Table of Contents

Missing "Peace" of the Puzzle 9
   By Alicia Moss

Peace in this World Today 13
   By Andrea Leeder

Turn Your Eyes Upon Jesus 17
   By Crystal Aldridge

The Prince Determines Your Peace 21
   By Kim Thompson

Peace in the Valley of the Shadow of Death 25
   By Anja Meyer

Peace: Security from Above 29
   By Belinda Young

The Peaceful Sleep of Those Who Dwell in Safety . . . 35
   By Misty Wells

Peace in the Midst of Every Trial 39
   By Marie Barron

A God Who is Peace 43
   By Kay Reese

Recipe for Peace 47
   By Rikki Beth Poindexter

Peace in Christ, not in Circumstances 51
   By Lisa Petersen

Peace in My Daily Life 55
   By Elizabeth Garrett

Having Peace While Being Single 59
   By Jenny Young

Peace and Provision 63
   By Grace Shiflett

Personal Responsibility in Peace 69
   By Christy Tadlock

The Prescription for Perfect Peace 75
   By Lydia L. Riley

Straight 'A' Student? 79
   By Nicole Redmon

Peace in Uncertainty 83
   By Rainy Lehman

A Peaceful Haven 87
   By Coretta Gomes

"Good but Lost" 93
   By Deborah South

What Brings Us Peace? 97
   By Lois Van Zee

Lay Me Down in Peace 101
   By Debra Lynn Birner

One Thing is Needful 105
   By Sarah Russell

Where to Find Peace 109
   By Sharon Garrett

Peace in a Crazy World 113
   By Kate Ledbetter

Left with the "Peaces" 117
   By Cherith Shiflett

Peace in Decision Making 123
   By Hannah Kasprzyk

The Ornament of a Peaceful Spirit 127
   By Susan Hutchens

Peace is the "Piece to the Puzzle" 131
   By Catherine Aylor

What the Lost are Looking For: Peace 137
   By Hannah Suttle

Peace...Even There 141
   By Kelly Byrley

Dedication

To those faithful ladies who have known the hurt or lose of a friend, thank you for never quitting but for teaching us by example how to build godly friendships.

Introduction

Our world screams chaos. Busy schedules. Deadlines. Appointments. Flashy signs. Banners. Parties. Events. Anxiety medications. Psychologists. Therapy. The list goes on and on. Seems we can't go one day without hearing about someone's childhood trauma and anxiety attacks. Although some cases surrounding these topics are valid, the devil has used these terms and "conditions" to take away from the peace that God, His salvation, and His Word can bring to a believer.

These stresses take a toll on relationships. Husbands and wives argue over credit card debt. Wives stress over the unknowns of their husband's job situation. Parents and children become overwhelmed with hectic schedules. Moms get anxious when toddler spills and baby cries are all that the day held for them.

The church isn't immune to the disunity that backbiting, lying, and pride can bring on, causing chaos as well. Ladies bicker about who was and was not invited to the baby shower. Petty arguments spring forth when feelings are hurt, and friendships are ruined when gossip spreads because of misinformation.

None of this is peaceful. But that's Satan's plan. He distracts our hearts and minds from the Truth of God's Word. A Truth that says, "And the peace of God, which passeth all understanding, shall keep your hearts and minds through Christ Jesus," Philippians 4:7. A Truth that says, "endeavouring to keep the unity of the Spirit in the bond of peace," Ephesians 4:3.

The word "peace" encompasses topics ranging from overcoming stress and anxiety to clinging to it during a dark trial to keeping unity in relationships. This devotional covers all of these topics in some way. Take the next thirty-one days and let the Lord work in your heart in this area of peace.

Missing "Peace" of the Puzzle

By Alicia Moss

Finally, brethren, whatsoever things are true, whatsoever things are honest, whatsoever things are just, whatsoever things are pure, whatsoever things are lovely, whatsoever things are of good report; if there be any virtue, and if there be any praise, think on these things.

Philippians 4:8

Recently, my love for puzzles has been ignited again. The challenge of putting pieces together to make a beautiful picture is rewarding. I also love the quiet time it brings. The tranquility of finding the perfect piece after skimming through the pieces over and over is exhilarating. There have been many nights while working on a puzzle that the Lord just came beside me and made Himself real. One night, I was thinking how wonderful it was to have some alone time, no music, no talking, no background noise, and then He showed up and began to show me how He has blessed me in so many ways. Later, I thought, "Wow! God has all the pieces of my life in His hands." Thank you, Lord! He knows what piece comes next to make a beautiful picture for Him.

Life can have so many pieces. There are pieces of success, failure, discouragement, church, and family. There are puzzle pieces that bring His peace, however there may be a couple of rough pieces that will not produce peace in our lives. I want and need peace. As a woman, many times I fret and worry. I try to find the solutions to the problems and trials we face.

Many times I am reminded that it is not self that brings peace. Peace only comes from Him. John 16:33: "These things have I spoken unto you, that in me ye might have peace...." He only gives peace. Write the fret down and give it to Him. Tell your worries to Him and then give it to Him. Refuse to fall in the flesh's trap of picking the worry back up. Think of Him. Philippians 4:8: "Finally, brethren, whatsoever things are true, whatsoever things are honest, whatsoever things are just, whatsoever things are pure, whatsoever things are lovely, whatsoever things are of good report; if there be any virtue, and if there be any praise, think on these things."

Are you picking up a "piece" of life that you are trying to make fit into God's Puzzle Design for your life? You may be thinking, but God if only I had ____, I would be at peace. Or so often I tell myself the lie, keep the house in order, and you will have more peace. No, God's perfect puzzle pieces of peace only come from Him. No human, no job, no church, no ministry will bring peace.

1. Love Him
2. Read About Him
3. Talk to Him

He has the perfect puzzle "piece" that will bring you peace. Determine in your heart to submit to the "pieces" He has designed for your life. He will give you peace!

peace

Notes:

Prayer Requests:

Peace in this World Today

By Andrea Leeder

Peace, I leave with you, my peace I give unto you; not as the world giveth, give I unto you. Let not your heart be troubled, neither let it be afraid.

John 14:27

With all the uncertainty today, it is easy to get upset and worried about everything – all of the sickness going around, the economy and unrest in our nation, the violence and crime, drugs and wickedness of this world, those that are changing their beliefs and throwing in the towel on standards and godliness. It can be very disappointing, discouraging, and worrisome. If we're not careful, we begin to take our eyes off of God and fix them on all of what's going on around us. We become a nervous wreck!

I would encourage you to focus on God's Word. Cling to the One who can give us peace and joy even through the hardest of times. Meditate on His Word and memorize scripture.

When everything seems upside down, we can experience a peace that the world could never have. We have access to God's Word!

We can pray anytime we want! The world has to look to drugs and alcohol and wicked living to try to find peace, and still, it is never found. We have our Heavenly Father Who loves us, comforts us, and gives us a peace that sometimes can't be explained.

Isaiah 26:3, "Thou wilt keep him in perfect peace, whose mind is stayed on thee: because he trusteth in thee." God knows exactly what is going on around us, and He is allowing these things to happen. He protects those that are His and we can rest assured that He will be all that we need to get us through these unsettling times.

Ask the Lord to help you not to worry, and pray more than you worry. We know that someday, He's going to make all things right. If you've accepted Christ in your heart, you can have peace that someday you will spend forever in heaven with Him! Psalm 37:11, "But the meek shall inherit the earth; and shall delight themselves in the abundance of peace."

My challenge to you is when you get worried about all that is going on around you, bury yourself in prayer and God's Word. Only He can give you a peace that passes all understanding! He will be your rock and shelter from the storm! Colossians 3:15, "And let the peace of God rule in your hearts, to the which also ye are called in one body; and be ye thankful." Psalm 4:8, "I will both lay me down in peace, and sleep: for thou, Lord, only makest me dwell in safety."

peace

Notes:

Prayer Requests:

Turn Your Eyes Upon Jesus

By Crystal Aldridge

I will lift up mine eyes unto the hills, from whence cometh my help. My help cometh from the LORD, which made heaven and earth.

Psalm 121: 1-2

I love to travel back in my mind to the night the Lord saved me almost twenty-six years ago. It was the first service of the week at a youth camp I reluctantly attended. I was seventeen years old. God's man preached a message on "The High Cost of Low Living." The Holy Spirit dealt with my heart, and I turned to Jesus in faith and repentance. The heavy burden of my sin lifted. What peace flooded my soul!

Just as I turned to Jesus that night and experienced the wonderful peace He brings, the answer is still the same today when my peace is disrupted. I must turn to Him! Discontentment, a critical spirit, self-love, and a distracted mind are just a few examples of peace disruptors. When our minds are filled with negative thinking, things that should bring us delight bring feelings of dread.

We read about Mary and Martha in Luke 10:38-42. Mary is found sitting at the feet of Jesus, her heart turned toward Him, listening to His word. The thought of this scene that day brings peace to my heart. Martha was busy serving. She was gracious to open her home, and I'm sure she felt honored to serve Jesus and the others that day, but Martha had a distracted mind. She began to feel sorry for herself, and what should have brought her great delight was now dread. Jesus gently rebuked her, reminding her she was troubled about many things. He pointed out that Mary chose to do what was needful.

When minors become majors while serving, our minds become consumed with thoughts that hinder our peace. What should be a blessing to us and others becomes a heavy load when we lose a heavenly perspective. We must heed God's Word, accept His loving rebuke as Martha did, and allow our peace to be restored.

Examine your heart. Can you identify peace disruptors? Turn to Jesus, and let Him restore your peace of mind. Isaiah 26:3 says, "Thou wilt keep him in perfect peace, whose mind is stayed on thee: because he trusteth in thee."

The Prince Determines Your Peace

By Kim Thompson

Thou wilt keep him in perfect peace, whose mind is stayed on thee: because he trusteth in thee.

Isaiah 26:3

Please don't be confused by the title! I'm not referring to your flesh and bone Prince Charming – although he's certinly capable of adding to your peace! (Hopefully, he doesn't rob you of peace!) I'm talking about the daily choice you make in your mind to either trust the Prince of Peace – your Savior Jesus Christ – or to let your mind fixate on the chaos that the prince of the power of the air – Satan – has designed for the day. Romans 8:6 says, "For to be carnally minded is death; but to be spiritually minded is life and peace."

As long as we have breath, there will be trials and tribulations – imagined or real! That perfect "peace of God, which passeth all understanding" was never meant as a promise to fix everyone and everything around us; it fixes us. This peace keeps "your hearts and minds through Christ Jesus." Peace or vexation of spirit lies within your power. To whom will you yield? To the lovely Prince of Peace or to the prince of this world? Dear lady, choose wisely; your mental health and future usefulness to a worthy God depends on your selection!

> "For to be carnally minded is death;
> but to be spiritually minded is life and peace."
> - Romans 8:6

peace

Notes:

Prayer Requests:

Peace in the Valley of the Shadow of Death

By Anja Meyer

Yea, though I walk through the valley of the shadow of death, I will fear no evil: for thou art with me; thy rod and thy staff they comfort me.

Psalm 23:4

The first time I read John Bunyan's *Pilgrim's Progress*, the description of how Christian and Hopeful went through the River Jordan made a huge impression on me. I was greatly encouraged by the help the Lord gives when it is time to go through death unto the Celestial City. Only years later I was to walk through the valley of the shadow of death and experience the truth of the verse above. May I suggest the following for when you walk through this valley:

1. FIND COMFORT IN THE SCRIPTURES.

The Psalms are wonderful to provide hope and comfort, and Job is great to offer perspective and gratefulness. However, in the hospital, ill with sepsis, I was so afraid of dying, not because I wasn't sure of my salvation, but because of my five young children, that I was unable to read the scriptures. My dear husband read the scriptures to me, and it was a great comfort. At my request, he repeatedly read the account of Peter attempting to walk on the water. I imagined myself in Peter's shoes – sinking while my eyes were on the waves around me. The only thing Peter could do was cry out to his Saviour. But when he saw the wind boisterous, he was afraid; and beginning to sink, he cried, saying, "Lord, save me." And immediately Jesus stretched forth his hand, and caught him (Matthew 14:30 – 31a).

2. CRY OUT TO THE LORD.

Our loving Lord is faithful to hear and save us. When my darling baby boy, Judah, passed away after only 20 weeks in the womb, my heart was broken, and I was desperate for comfort from the Lord. One night my husband encouraged me to pray aloud with him, but I couldn't string together a sensible prayer. The only thing that escaped my lips was a cry to the Lord for help. Over and over, I cried out to Him. He was there with me, and He caught me. Since that moment, the most wonderful peace flooded my soul. "And the peace of God, which passeth all understanding, shall keep your hearts and minds through Christ Jesus," Philippians 4:7.

3. REST IN THE LORD.

When my mum passed away unexpectedly, I could rest in the Lord. I knew from experience how the Lord is with me in the valley of the shadow of death and how He will comfort me. Faith is not blind, our pastor always says. It is the belief and trust that comes from experience. We can look forward with confidence, remembering how the LORD has been faithful throughout the good times, but especially through the difficult times. "And let the peace of God rule in your hearts," Colossians 3:15a.

peace

Notes:

Prayer Requests:

Peace: Security from Above

By Belinda Young

My little children, let us love not in word, neither in tongue; but in deed and in truth.

I John 3:18

If it be possible, as much as lieth in you, live peaceably with all men.

Romans 12:18

In your life, you will meet contentious and angry people. They are obstinate and nigh impossible to get along with. If you do not have to live with them, be thankful -- be thankful for the family you have, treasure the blessing you have, and treat them in kindness.

Sometimes this obstinate and angry person is someone in your household that you have to deal with on a daily basis. If this is someone you are teaching or someone under you, do not allow such behavior. If you do not like your children, nobody else is going to like them either. Teach them, instruct them, correct them, and don't leave them alone with anybody until they have gotten rid of the obstinate attitude.

Other times, this is someone to whom you are supposed to submit to. There is never peace because they are constantly angry and finding

"Let your conversation be without covetousness; and be content with such things as ye have: for he hath said, I will never leave thee, nor forsake thee."

- Hebrews 13:5

fault with everyone. You are provoked to anger, but if you respond in anger, it just gets worse. Or you just give in to the pressure and condone "wrong" to make peace There are battles you must choose. Some battles are not worth fighting – they are silly and short-lived. Other battles are of great importance – battles regarding principles in the Word of God. These are battles that are not to be overlooked or swapped for peace. They are not won by anger or in-your-face conversations. They are won by your faithful living for God. It is something you will have to do – many times all alone.

You may have to keep your mouth shut, or you may have to firmly say, "I will or I will not do this thing because I love the Lord, and His Word clearly teaches for this or against this." You will need wisdom from the Lord to know the right time when "to do" or when "to say" something. James 1:5 says, "If any of you lack wisdom, let him ask of God, that giveth to all men liberally, and upbraideth not; and it shall be given him." Though the atmosphere around you is full of turmoil, you can have a peace in your heart when you are loving the Lord Jesus, feeding on His Word throughout the day, and praying for those in your life who so desperately need help.

This is not something that anybody feels they can master. It is a situation that many have to live in. Sometimes, it is a spouse that you never would have dreamed would have been that way. Or it is a defiant parent of a young person who has come to know the Lord as their

Savior. Live for the Lord; love Him with all your heart. Pray that He will give you the love for this person and the wisdom to help this one though they are "over you." They may never overcome their anger and bitterness. But you do not have to live with anger and bitterness in your heart. Why would you want to be miserable?

God gives peace in the midst of storms. Claim His Word and bask in his goodness, though the billows rage. Be content with the little things – which are great things with contentment. Hebrews 13:5 says, "Let your conversation be without covetousness; and be content with such things as ye have: for he hath said, I will never leave thee, nor forsake thee."

peace

Notes:

Prayer Requests:

The Peaceful Sleep of Those Who Dwell in Safety

By Misty Wells

---

*I will both lay me down in peace, and sleep:
for thou, Lord, only makest me dwell in safety.*

Psalms 4:8

One of the most precious experiences of being a mother is watching the peaceful sleep of my babies. I love to see their little sleepy eyes gently close as they drift off. Our daughter, who is four months old, sleeps especially well when her belly is full and the atmosphere around her is warm, calm, and safe. The older two need a little more assurance. So, we discuss the fact that dinosaurs are extinct, and bears are more afraid of us than we are of them. This lasts for a few minutes before we pray and turn the lights out. If I can convince them that they are in a safe place in the care of Mom and Dad, they will sleep in peace.

Peaceful sleep is a blessing from the Lord. It's a time when, though we are completely unaware of what's going on around us, we trust that we are safe and well. The psalmist David says in Psalms 4:8, "I will both lay me down in peace, and sleep: for thou, Lord, only makest me dwell in safety." The acts of David's rebellious son, Absalom, had forced David to flee for his life (II Samuel 15:13-14). The hearts of the people who once loved him had turned to follow Absalom. In the eyes of man, David was far from being in a place of safety. How could he sleep in peace when his life was at stake?

Let's look closely at the verse. David says "I will both." So we see two things that he is going to do. He is going to first lay down in peace. If he had a cell phone, he would put it down. He has chosen to turn off the disturbing news of the day. Ladies, there is negativity all around us just waiting to steal our peaceful sleep. We must turn it off and lay down in peace. Secondly, he is going to sleep. If coffee were available, I'm sure he would've taken his last cup no later than 4:00 p.m. There are many practical things that we can implement to help us sleep well.

The greatest contribution to David's peaceful sleep was that he knew he was dwelling in safety. The Bible says, "for thou, Lord, only makest me dwell in safety." In the worst of circumstances, we can sleep in peace knowing that in the will of God, we are only dwelling in safety. I agree with Charles Spurgeon when he said, "The sovereignty of God is the pillow upon which the child of God rests his head at night, giving perfect peace."

We are living in uncertain days. Don't let them keep you awake. God is still on His throne. He is still in control, and you are safe in His care. Sleep in peace, my friend.

peace

Notes:

Prayer Requests:

Peace in the Midst of Every Trial

By Marie Barron

To appoint unto them that mourn in Zion, to give unto them beauty for ashes, the oil of joy for mourning, the garment of praise for the spirit of heaviness; that they might be called trees of righteousness, the planting of the Lord, that he might be glorified.

Isaiah 61:3

Through trials, I have always wanted to come through at the end changed for the positive to glorify God. My lifelong prayer has been, "Lord, please let me learn the first time what you are trying to teach me through this trial. I do not want to go through this again." The Lord has truly been with me through every trial that I have ever faced.

Early in my marriage when I lost my first baby, I had no idea how to make it through. I prayed for understanding, but I did not demand an answer. The Lord carried me through but chose not to give me answers. He wanted me to trust Him (Proverbs 3:5-6). Later, He gave me a healthy baby boy (Psalm 37:4).

As time went on and my faith and trust grew, God had another much more difficult trial for me to go through. I was expecting a set of twins and we were very excited! Our family had prayed for this. However, the twins died. The doctors felt that it was safer for me to carry the twins until my body went into labor on its own instead of forcing me to go into labor. During the weeks that passed, my husband and little boy could not be close to me or hug me because they said, "I was like a casket carrying around their babies." I was broken and so heavy--hearted that I could barely utter the hurt in my heart. It was then that the verses in Romans 8:26-27 became so real to me.

After a few weeks, God led us to another doctor. This doctor was just coming back from a mental health leave due to his wife going through a very similar trial. This doctor understood the emotional turmoil my family was in, and he decided it was more important to our emotional health to go ahead and force my body into labor instead of waiting for my body to begin labor on its own. (Praise the Lord!) Not only did God send me to this doctor, but He gave me a peace that passeth all understanding. I felt God wrap me in His arms and hold me, giving me the greatest of all hugs. I clung to Philippians 4:7 and Psalm 91:4.

I always enjoy a hug, but this was beyond anything I had ever felt. God knew how much I needed a hug at this time. Once again God not only held me and carried me through this trial, but he used this trial to save my mom. I had been praying for nineteen years for my mom to be saved. Never stop praying (Philippians 4:6-7)!

The Lord then gave me the wonderful blessing of being able to serve Him together with my mom for twenty years before taking my mom home to heaven, an answered prayer for my heart's desire (Philippians 37:4). "The Lord is my rock, and my fortress, and my deliverer; my God, my strength, in whom I will trust; my buckler, and the horn of my salvation, my high tower," Psalm 18:2.

peace

Notes:

Prayer Requests:

A God Who is Peace

By Kay Reese

...and on earth peace, good will toward men.

Luke 2:14

These words were heralded out to some frightened, lowly shepherds one very special night. Heavenly messengers praised God and told them to fear not. What they had longed for all their life had come! Peace! Jesus, the Prince of Peace, brought to all men goodwill and set at one again God and man. He is the key to complete rest! The essence of all that it is! He can speak as in Mark 4:39 and all is quiet and still. Jesus is our peace according to Ephesians 2:14. He causes turmoil and fears to flee. He banishes doubt, despair, and depression. His peace fills our lives where sin once controlled us and separated us from a Holy God.

I was not raised in church. Relatives occasionally tried to get me to go. There were times I would go to Bible school at nearby churches. I knew of Jesus and that He died on a cross from pictures I had seen. I did not know He died for me, nor that He was alive. I had not learned much about Him at all! I remember asking myself, why was I here and why had I been born? I had such an emptiness inside! I sought whatever could give me rest, but nothing worked. But, one day He who is Peace made Himself known to me! He brought an end to the craziness in my life. I have never been the same! Now I can walk each day knowing He has all things in control. When we have no peace, no purpose in this life, He is but a call away. He grants to us what we don't know we were even searching for.

Jesus loves us so much! Lord, thank you for coming to this earth for the goodwill of all of us here. Help us to share what we know with others so they may know You, who is Peace.

> His peace fills our lives where sin once controlled us and separated us from a Holy God.

Recipe for Peace

By Rikki Beth Poindexter

Be careful for nothing; but in every thing by prayer and supplication with thanksgiving let your requests be made known unto God. And the peace of God, which passeth all understanding, shall keep your hearts and minds through Christ Jesus Finally, brethren, whatsoever things are true, whatsoever things are honest, whatsoever things are just, whatsoever things are pure, whatsoever things are lovely, whatsoever things are of good report; if there be any virtue, and if there be any praise, think on these things. Those things, which ye have both learned, and received, and heard, and seen in me, do: and the God of peace shall be with you.

Philippians 4:6-9

Don't be anxious. Pray about everything. Be thankful! The peace of God, which is superior, will come from that. That peace will help guard and protect our hearts and minds - which is where we can really mess up peace. Then we are given a list of things to think on. Follow the list! Memorize it!

If we will do these things that Paul tells us about, again he says, we will have the peace of God. For me who loves checklists, it seems so simple.

So why isn't it simple? We do not control our thoughts. Everything Paul is instructing us on happens in the mind. He is even telling us what to think on: almost a fool-proof recipe. We simply do not have control over our minds! DISCIPLINE is the key!

We are living in the day when information is so accessible. We have all of these tools and information galore at our fingertips. We are putting in and studying. What are we doing with the information? Here in this passage, we have the recipe for peace. It is our job and responsibility to do it, not anyone else's.

II Corinthians 10:5, "Casting down imaginations, and every high thing that exalteth itself against the knowledge of God, and bringing into captivity every thought to the obedience of Christ."

Paul is talking about strongholds in verse 4 and goes right to the mind and controls our thoughts! This is vital to our peace. Do you want peace? Control your thoughts! This takes the most discipline! We know, that without control, our minds can be as wild as we will let them, which will steal and rob our peace.

peace

Notes:

Prayer Requests:

Peace in Christ, not in Circumstances

By Lisa Petersen

Jesus told His disciples before he left this earth, Peace I leave with you, my peace I give unto you: not as the world giveth, give I unto you. Let not your heart be troubled, neither let it be afraid.

John 14:27

It is very easy to condition ourselves to look at circumstances to determine whether we have peace, but what about when circumstances are in upheaval and everything goes wrong? Can I still have peace? Is it any peace at all that can't endure when circumstances change; when they are no longer conducive to living peacefully?

The peace the world gives is the peace of circumstance. Jesus said He came not to bring that kind of peace. His peace rules in the heart, regardless of circumstance. Christ's peace is available to a heart tempted to be troubled and fearful.

Peace is the fruit of the Holy Spirit. God's peace is sustained by the Word of God. We can have peace in relationships, in our homes, our churches, and with our community. We can have peace in the middle of a storm when we keep our eyes on Him. Peace is not the absence of trouble; it is the presence of the Savior.

There will be many things in our life that will cause us to lose peace; the loss of a job, the loss of friends, the loss of loved ones, and the list could go on. But if we are looking at those things to bring us peace, we will eventually be disappointed.

We must look at the peace that only Christ can bring, whether circumstances are good or not. We should get into the Word of God, see what it says about having His peace, take Him at His Word, and put our complete trust in Him.

As the song "Peace in Christ" says, "He gives us hope when hope is gone. He gives us strength when we can't go on. He gives us shelter in the storms of life. There's no peace on earth; there is peace in Christ."

Peace in My Daily Life

By Elizabeth Garrett

Now it came to pass, as they went, that he entered into a certain village: and a certain woman named Martha received him into her house. And she had a sister called Mary, which also sat at Jesus' feet, and heard his word. But Martha was cumbered about much serving, and came to him, and said, Lord, dost thou not care that my sister hath left me to serve alone? bid her therefore that she help me. And Jesus answered and said unto her, Martha, Martha, thou art careful and troubled about many things: But one thing is needful: and Mary hath chosen that good part, which shall not be taken away from her.

Luke 10:38-42

We lead very busy, even hectic lives with a million things to do and not enough time to do it all. There are so many distractions and needs vying for our attention. If we are not careful, we can easily become overwhelmed by this busy-ness. That is where we find Martha in Luke 10. Truthfully, I find that I relate very well to Martha and her situation, her frustration, and her lack of peace. There was no issue with her work or her service; the issue was that she had lost her peace in the midst of it all. Verse 40 says that she was "cumbered about" (distracted, over-occupied); and Jesus told her in verse 41 that she was "careful (anxious) and troubled about many things." Martha had allowed her circumstances to steal her peace.

This leads us to ask, "How can I keep a heart of peace in the midst of a hectic, busy life?" We find the answer by observing Mary, Martha's sister. There are three key points that we find in these verses.

First, Mary sat at Jesus' feet. He was her focus, and He had her undivided attention. Apparently, Mary was so tuned into what Jesus was teaching that she did not even notice her sister's struggles or frustrations. If we are to keep a heart of peace, we must keep Jesus as our focus. Isaiah 26:3 says, "Thou wilt keep him in perfect peace, whose mind is stayed on thee: because he trusteth in thee." The Lord promises perfect peace to those whose mind is stayed on (propped or leaned upon) Him.

Second, Mary heard Jesus' words. She was listening to what Jesus had to say. Later when Mary anointed the feet of Jesus with the precious ointment, Jesus said, "...against the day of my burying hath she kept this" (John 12:7). She had understood Jesus' purpose on this earth when his other disciples had not. How? She was actively listening to His words. Psalm 119:165 says, "Great peace have they which love thy law: and nothing shall offend them." Great peace is promised to those who love God's Word. If I love His Word, I will read, study, and memorize those Words.

Third, Mary communed with Jesus. She had a personal, close relationship with Him. It is interesting that Mary went to the sepulchre to anoint Jesus' body, and she was the first person to whom He appeared. Jesus called her by name, and she knew His voice! This communion comes through prayer. Philippians 4:6-7 tells us, "Be careful (anxious) for nothing; but in every thing by prayer and supplication with thanksgiving let your requests be made known unto God. And the peace of God, which passeth all understanding, shall keep your hearts and minds through Christ Jesus." There is an inexplicable peace given through prayer.

When we attend to these "basics" of the Christian life, how profoundly we are affected! We can find and keep a peaceful heart in our daily lives!

peace

Notes:

Prayer Requests:

Having Peace While Being Single

By Jenny Young

Thou wilt keep him in perfect peace, whose mind is stayed on thee: because he trusteth in thee.

Isaiah 26:3

The word "peace" carries with it the meaning of "freedom from agitation or disturbance by the passions, as from fear, terror, anger, anxiety or the like; quietness of mind; tranquility; calmness; quiet of conscience." The word peace is mentioned in four hundred verses in the Bible. Peace must be important to God if it is mentioned that many times.

When I got saved, God gave me a peace that passes all understanding; however, I must have peace about God's will for my life. God's plan for some is to marry, but for others, it is to remain single. I may never get married, but right now I know I'm in God's will for my life. This does not mean that I do not struggle some days with being single. On these days, God reassures me I am in His will, and He re-establishes His peace in my heart.

I used to think that my life did not have much value or meaning because I was single. I soon came to realize that my life can bring just as much honor and glory to God as any other Christian lady. However, I must be willing to let Him use me as I am. God made me, a single lady, with a special purpose in mind.

For instance, I do not have any children of my own, but God has blessed me with children. He has allowed my life to affect others by helping a missionary family and by teaching Sunday School. The Lord has also blessed me with a niece and a nephew and adopted nieces and nephews. Being a part of these children's lives has brought me great joy and happiness.

One day in 2012, my pastor gave me a book to read entitled "The Abundant Single Life" by a single lady named Ms. Joanna Jackson. Little did he know that I was struggling and needed help in this area of my life. I believe I cried through most of the book. I could relate to what she wrote, and I wanted to have the peace that she had about being single. I know God used that book in my life to help me have peace with being single. (If you are struggling with being single or if you are married and want to understand a single lady better, I would recommend that you read this book.)

I would like to share with you some verses I have written in the back of my Bible. I refer to these verses often, and I pray they are a blessing to you: Deuteronomy 33:27; Isaiah 41:10; I Peter 5:7; Deuteronomy 31:6; Hebrews 13:5 and Psalm 62:8. Perfect peace comes from keeping your mind on God. God can give you peace while being single. Just ask Him!

Peace and Provision

By Grace Shiflett

Be careful for nothing; but in every thing by prayer and supplication with thanksgiving let your request be made known unto God. And the peace of God, which passeth all understanding, shall keep your hearts and minds through Christ Jesus.

Philippians 4:6,7

I'm going to share a story that comes to mind every time I think of God's peace. As far back as my memory takes me, I have known this story of peace – one that my dad would share many times. I've seen tears swell up in his eyes through the years while relaying these memories. Maybe you will be encouraged through this testimony of peace and provision.

It was the year 1975. My dad had moved our family of five at the time (my sister and I were not yet born) from Milledgeville, GA to Greenville, SC to attend Bible College. Upon this move, my dad struggled to find a job. They were down to $10 and a case of homemade jelly my great-grandmother

had sent with them when they moved. There were bills to be paid and a family to feed. Dad and Mom prayed about it and agreed they would take the $10, go to the local bread store, and buy all the bread they

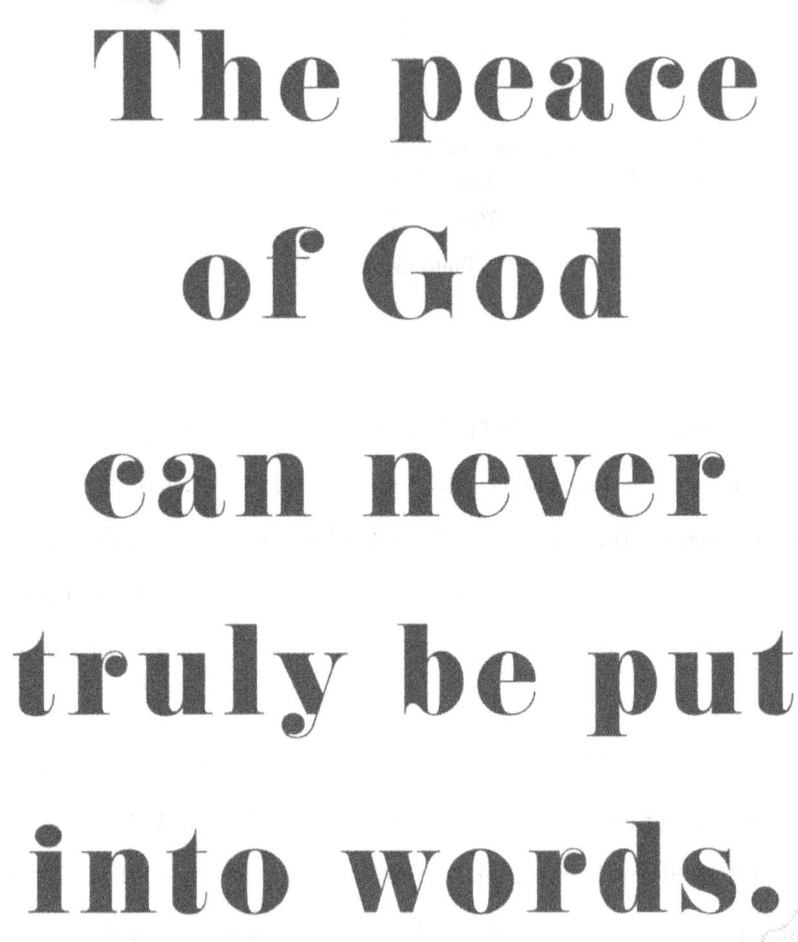

The peace of God can never truly be put into words.

could with the money they had. So that is what they did. Dad was sure to insert somewhere around this part of the story how happy he and my mom were during all of this during a time when happiness would not be the emotions you would expect someone in their situation to have.

On Saturday night, he said God gave him peace – no doubt unexplainable peace. Hewas just sure this peace was God letting him know that first thing Monday he would find a job! On Sunday morning, he walked into church with peace flooding his soul. Wouldn't you know the special music for that service was a soloist who sang "Peace, Peace, Wonderful Peace." He said it's the first time he had shouted in church!

Monday came with much anticipation as he left early in search of a job. By late afternoon, he still came up with nothing. He went home discouraged and told my mom he was going to take a nap on the couch. He wasn't asleep long when he was awakened by a very excited wife shaking his arm and rejoicing. You see, the mail had come and there was a stack of envelopes and each one had a piece of money, all different amounts from all different sources. It was enough to take care of everything they needed, plus some! He would recall in one of those envelopes, one lady had gotten an inheritance and wanted to give some of it to them. The peace he felt thinking a job would be the solution was just God all along wanting to show him a greater, unexplainable miracle of peace and provision. Oh, by the way, the Lord gave my dad a job on Tuesday!

My dad got saved on March 8, 1970. He got saved because he said he longed for peace – the peace he knew only God could give – lasting peace, come what may. Maybe the peace of God can never truly be put into words. You just feel it and know that this peace only comes to those who are a child of God.

I will close with the lyrics to this beautiful hymn. It's no wonder all my life this song is and will always be one of my favorites:

Peace, Peace, Wonderful Peace

Far away in the depths of my spirit tonight
Rolls a melody sweeter than psalm
In celestial-like strains it unceasingly falls
O'er my soul like an infinite calm

Peace, peace, wonderful peace
Coming down from the Father above
Sweep over my spirit forever, I pray
In fathomless billows of love

Ah, soul are you here without comfort and rest
Marching down the rough pathway of time?
Make Jesus your friend ere the shadows grow dark
O accept of this sweet peace so sublime

Peace, peace, wonderful peace
Coming down from the Father above
Sweep over my spirit forever, I pray
In fathomless billows of love

Peace, peace, wonderful peace
Coming down from the Father above
Sweep over my spirit forever, I pray
In fathomless billows of love

Personal Responsibility in Peace

By Christy Tadlock

If it be possible, as much as lieth in you, live peaceably with all men.

Romans 12:18

Let him eschew evil, and do good; let him seek peace, and ensue it.

1 Peter 3:11

Follow peace with all men, and holiness, without which no man shall see the Lord.

Hebrews 12:14

Are you a bystander when it comes to your peace? Absolutely not! On a daily basis, we make choices that impact our peace. All three of the verses above refer to my personal responsibility in seeking and following peace. If I am commanded to seek and follow peace, then the opposite is what I should not do. I should not seek conflict. I should not follow discord. Stop and think about your personal responsibility in your peace.

1) Am I involved in sins of commission (actions)?
2) Am I involved in sins of omission (failing to act)?
3) Am I reacting to the actions of others haphazardly?
4) Am I being prideful?
5) Am I involved in close friendships with self-consume people (a.k.a drama seekers)?

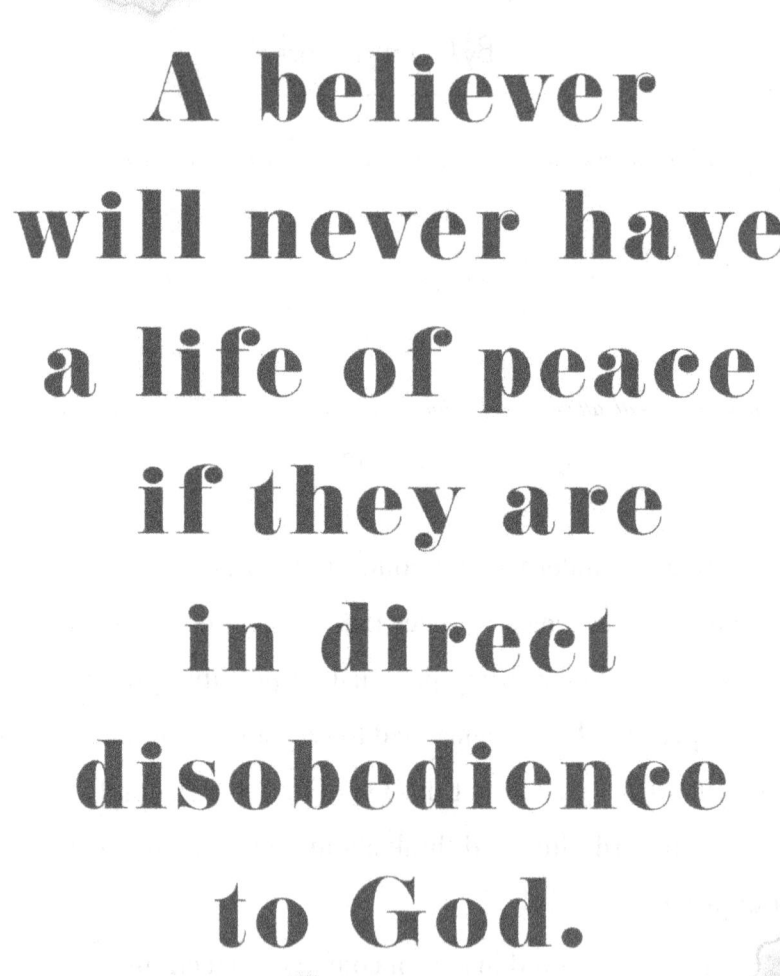

A believer will never have a life of peace if they are in direct disobedience to God.

If your answer is yes to any of the questions above, then you are destroying your ability to have peace. (Obviously, I'm not referring to the peace you received through salvation. That's purely a gift of God!) I'm referencing the day-to-day peace of living a life focused on God and obedience to God. Take ownership of your peace.

If you are saved and living in sin, you will not have peace. If you choose to not read your Bible and pray daily, you will not have peace. Why? Because you are living in direct rebellion of God's Word. A believer will never have a life of peace if they are in direct disobedience to God. If you immediately respond to the actions of others without prayerful thought and guidance, you will not have peace. News flash, y'all, I absolutely unequivocally cannot control anything that others do. But I can absolutely, unequivocally control my reaction to what they do. If I can't learn to control my temper, tongue, emotions, and attitude, I will not have peace - that's not even because of anybody else, it's because of me.

I disgust myself when I look back on my reactions with embarrassment, worry, and condemnation. I need to be able to end each day having peace with God because I responded in mature wisdom, as well as peace with myself knowing I responded correctly.

If you are living a self-consumed life, you will never have peace. Why? Because the world will never revolve around you. You will never be at peace because it will never be all about you. Make it all about Jesus, and I promise you peace. Drama and peace rarely coexist. You will never be able to be besties with a drama seeker if you desire a life of peace. Be cordial, be friendly, but protect your peace.

A peaceful life doesn't equal a perfect life. A peaceful life does not even equate to a stress-free life. A peaceful life is going to sleep at night knowing I have been obedient to God and I behaved in such a way through the day that I can rest easy. Strive for peace with God and peace with yourself.

peace

Notes:

Prayer Requests:

The Prescription for Perfect Peace:
The Deepest Need and Desire of Every Human Heart

By Lydia L. Riley

Thou wilt keep him in perfect peace, whose mind is stayed on thee: because he trusteth in thee.

Isaiah 26:3

How good of our perfect God (Matthew 5:48) – Whose way is perfect (Psalm 18:30) - Who gives us perfect gifts (James 1:17) – to also provide for His creation to have "perfect peace"? As ladies, when we exclaim over a favored gift, we often squeal in delight, "I love it! It's perfect!" This is the kind of gift that God provides for His children – His peace is absolutely perfect. It is complete, it is not defective in any way!

The actual Hebrew word for *perfect* in Isaiah 26:3 is *Shalom*. Interestingly enough, the Hebrew word for *peace* is also *Shalom*! This verse is basically saying to us – "You keep him in peace, peace, whose mind is stayed on You!" *Shalom* is a large encompassing word for the good that comes to the person God favors.

The definition for *Shalom* is to be safe, sound, healthy, and signifies a sense of well-being and harmony both within and without – completeness, wholeness, peace, health, welfare, safety, soundness, tranquility, prosperity, fullness, rest, harmony – the absence of agitation or discord, a state of restful calm without anxiety or stress. This *Shalom* peace, this perfect peace that we have in Christ, implies much more than just an end of hostility – this is God's special word for wholeness and goodness and total satisfaction in life. As seen in John 10:10, Jesus promises this very concept of abundant life. He is our Shalom! He is our Peace (Ephesians 2:14-18).

The definition of "stay" is: to remain; to continue; to abide; to stop; to stand still; to dwell; to rest; to rely; to confide in; and to trust. When one's mind and thoughts are leaning on Jesus, centered on Him, trusting in Him, remaining and abiding on the faithful Saviour instead of themselves or their problems, then there is perfect peace. Why? Because "he trusteth in thee." I love the King James Bible and this word "trusteth" (this tense of the verb carries with it the essence of a continuing action). In other words, I am presently trusting and will continue to trust in Him. This gives my heart perfect peace!

When abiding and trusting, you can talk to Jesus about everything! "Be careful [anxious] for nothing, but in every thing by prayer and supplication with thanksgiving let your requests be made known unto God. And the peace of God which passeth all understanding, shall keep your hearts and minds through Christ Jesus." Philippians 4:6-7

Shalom my friend; rest in Jesus today. Keep your thoughts stayed on Him. Continue to trust in Him. He is our Peace, our Perfect Peace!

peace

Notes:

Prayer Requests:

Straight 'A' Student?

By Nicole Redmon

And that ye study to be quiet, and do your own business....

1Thessalonians 4:11a

Being a homeschool mom, studying has been part of my family's life for many years. If the kiddos made straight A's on their report card, we celebrated in special ways. Straight A's were always the goal, not always achieved, but still the aim of each child. When coming across this verse, the word "study" seemed to jump off the page at me. I decided to dig a little deeper into this truth.

Anyone who knows me personally, knows that I struggle with being quiet. My report cards throughout the years had "talks excessively" written in the teacher's notes. It is just not in my nature to be quiet. If you struggle with carrying on a conversation, I can carry your part and mine with ease. In other words, I can talk enough for two people. So, to "study to be quiet" was going to be a challenge for me indeed.

Let's unpack the first part of this verse by defining the word "study." Study means "earnestly endeavoring to accomplish a goal; to fix the mind closely on a subject; to dwell upon." When you think of peace, you will more than likely pair it with the word quiet. Have you ever said the phrase, "All I want is a little peace and quiet"?

To have that kind of peace, we must study for it. What are you studying? What grade would you achieve on your spiritual report card for being quiet? How are you at keeping peace and quiet at home? In your marriage? In your homeschooling? In your friendships? On the job? Would your teacher's notes include words like, "touchy, stubborn, opinionated, bossy, or quick-tempered"?

Ladies, we do not always have to have the last word in a discussion. We need to study the art of keeping our mouths closed and our hearts open. Would you sling insults to our Lord the same way you felt it extremely necessary to hurl at your husband? Would Jesus dismiss His children like we do when they make a mistake? Would the Lord find it essential to give His opinion on how the ladies at church should do those flowers in front of the pulpit?

We need to seek out ways to keep or maybe, at times, create a peaceful and quiet environment. Your motives will matter in what you say or don't say. The Holy Spirit will let you know when it is good to speak and when you should say nothing at all. Ecclesiastes 3:7, "…a time to keep silent, and a time to speak," reminds us of this. Make sure you can hear His voice. It will be exceptionally difficult to hear Him if you are constantly making noise yourself. Pray and ask the Lord how you should deal with that difficult coworker or if you should deal with them at all. Encourage that struggling child. Don't dangle past mistakes over their head. Aren't you glad our Lord does not do that to us? I believe it is safe to say that, more often than not, we should keep quiet. Study the Scriptures. Ask the Lord to help you in your "studies." Would you be a straight A student on your spiritual report card? If not, then we have some studying to do.

peace

Notes:

Prayer Requests:

Peace in Uncertainty

By Rainy Lehman

What time I am afraid, I will trust in thee.

Psalms 56:3

I am not a fan of change. With change comes the fear of the unknown, leaving me feeling out of control. I like schedules, traditions, and knowing what to expect. Unfortunately, change is a natural part of life, and it always will be. We are not omniscient like God so there will always be "unknowns" to face. However, as children of God, we have something that this world does not have; it is not something that the world can give, nor can it take it away. We have God's peace which "passeth all understanding"!

Everyone, lost and saved, will eventually face uncertain times. It can be uncertainties with your job, your health, your finances, your family, etc. The world "deals" with these uncertain times with drugs, alcohol, and anything else they can get their hands on to "escape" for a little while. Sadly, until they allow the Lord to take control of their life, they will desperately keep trying to take away that unsettled feeling. On the other hand, God's people have the Holy Ghost living on the inside who, so sweetly, will whisper "Peace, be still" to our hearts. When He does that, it doesn't matter what is going on in my life, a wave of peace floods my soul and I am reminded, like Job, "But He knoweth the way that I take; when he hath tried me, I shall come forth as gold" (Job 23:10).

No matter what time of uncertainty you are going through, hold fast to the promises of God! We can be encouraged by verses such as Isaiah 45:2, where He tells us that He will go before us "and make the crooked places straight." John 16:33 reminds us that we can be of good cheer because He has overcome the world. The entire chapter of Psalms 27 is David testifying that his heart will not fear (verse 1) and that he can be confident despite war rising against him (verse 3) because the Lord is his light and his salvation (verse 1).

Being saved will not exempt us from the uncertainties of this life, but being saved means that our world could crumble down around us and, while it may hurt for a while, we have this overwhelming and unexplainable peace. That same peace reminds us that "…weeping may endure for a night, but joy cometh in the morning." (Psalms 30:5). I wouldn't trade my best day as a lost person for my worst day as a saved child of God because there is nothing like that sweet peace that only the Lord can give!

A Peaceful Haven

By Coretta Gomes

For God is not the author of confusion, but of peace,....

I Corinthians 14:33a

Growing up in a missionary home was quite an adventure: flying as an eight-year-old was so cool (even though my parents didn't feel the same), meeting new people (I never met a stranger), learning a new language, seeing new places, and eating new foods, but at the same time, it was a challenge (especially for my parents). We were with each other 24/7. We were homeschooled and went everywhere together. We were each other's best friends.

My parents made it their goal to spend time with each one of us and to train us to be homemakers for our future families. Mom taught us how to cook from scratch (down to how to cut up a full chicken in pieces as that is all you could buy), sew, crochet, and clean. Dad tried to teach some of us girls how to drive a stick shift in the hills where we lived, do our own taxes, and balance a checkbook. Bless his heart, most of it went over our heads, but it was a great childhood. We learned to

Keep a peaceful environment by being careful what you allow in your home...

do everything you can imagine in the ministry, from teaching a Sunday School class, planning VBS, door-to-door witnessing, to cleaning the bathrooms. My parents made it seem so easy and effortless.

But those were not the most important things I learned growing up with the parents God gave me. I have realized through the years that I was blessed to grow up in a peaceful home. My parents made our home a peaceful haven! Now my family benefits from it. It might have seemed easy and effortless to a little child, but now that I have my own home, I realize that there were many factors behind the scenes to create that peaceful home environment.

I Corinthians 14:33 says, "God is not the author of confusion," the main word being "God." I remember my parents taking the time to spend with God in the early morning before starting their day. I know that there were times of frustration for my parents in trying to learn the language and culture and missing their family and American ways back home; however, that daily time spent with God allowed a frustrating situation or a down moment to be peacefully endured. They just trudged on! It taught me that I must make the time to spend with God every day so that when I am frustrated or overwhelmed, God's Word abiding in me gives me the ability to stop and think before blowing a gasket and saying something regrettable.

"God is not the author of confusion." Arguing was not a part of our home. If my parents disagreed on an issue, I was not aware of it. To me, they always seemed to agree on everything. I'm sure they had their disagreements, but we kids did not hear about it. Strive to be agreeable in your home, to keep the peace. Arguments are confusing and only cause strife and division. Stay in your prayer closet and ask the Lord to help you. Christian homes should not be a chaotic arguing match!

Keep a peaceful environment by being careful what you allow in your home in music, movies, and conversation. Growing up, we were not allowed to listen to whatever we wanted or to watch certain movies, even if other Christian families did. Family and friends thought we were weird, but those guidelines are implemented in our home today, and I am thankful for them. So much of the "entertainment" out there grieves the Holy Spirit and can cause chaos in your home and in the minds of your children. Be careful what you allow in your home!

Our homes should be a haven of peace for our families. In order to do that, we must have a few guidelines in our everyday lives. Make the time to spend with the Lord in Bible reading and prayer; ask Him to give you a peaceful home. Have guidelines in your home so that you can give the blessing of a peaceful home to your family. The world out there is a chaotic place of confusion and strife in all directions. Our homes should be a place of comfort for the soul, a peaceful Haven!

"Be careful for nothing; but in every thing by prayer and supplication with thanksgiving let your requests be made known unto God. And the peace of God, which passeth all understanding, shall keep your hearts and minds through Christ Jesus," Philippians 4:6-7.

peace

Notes:

Prayer Requests:

"Good but Lost"

By Deborah South

And the peace of God, which passeth all understanding, shall keep your hearts and minds through Christ Jesus.

Philippians 4:7

She was a good girl. She was. She never really gave her parents much trouble and if you asked her, she would proudly tell you she was good. When she was eight years old, all of her friends at church were going to the altar, so one Sunday she went as well. When she got home that day, her daddy asked her why she had gone to the altar, and knowing that the altar was a sacred place and you didn't play around at it, the only "good" reason she could think of was that she needed to be saved. She knew this answer would keep her out of trouble and please her family as well.

For several years, she lived with this false profession. She tried to do and say the things a Christian would do and say, but deep down there was no peace; just a lot of fear and pride. As she got older, the Lord started dealing with her heart and the lack of peace became very evident, especially at night. No one knew the fear that she had every night as she would go to bed. Was she going to die? What would happen then? There was no peace; only fear – the fear of death and not knowing where she was going. She had heard some of the best preaching in the world, but without conviction, there is no repentance. She had a great Christian family and her pastor was her dad. She proudly told herself how good she was, so surely she had to be saved. (It makes no difference what you tell yourself if it is not in accordance with the Word of God; the Bible is right and you are wrong.)

Finally, when she was in her early teens, her family went to a revival meeting because she wanted to go see friends; (her daddy had always said that if his children wanted to go to church, he would not hinder that). As the service began, the conviction of the Holy Spirit became so heavy in that young girl's heart that she didn't hear anything the preacher preached that night. She heard the Holy Spirit loud and clear. She knew that she could keep living in the fear of death and hell, or she could be saved. It was as if the Lord was telling her that this was her last opportunity to yield to Him. That night she was saved! The peace was there! "...the peace of God, which passeth all understanding..." - the peace that allows you to lay your head on your pillow at night and know, without a doubt, that you are on your way to Heaven not because of how good you are, but because of faith in what Jesus did on Calvary.

I know that this story of peace is true because it has been my story for over forty years.

What Brings Us Peace?

By Lois Van Zee

Thou wilt keep him in perfect peace, whose mind is stayed on thee: because he trusteth in thee.

Isaiah 26:3

One of the definitions of peace that I found is a state of tranquility, quiet, or calmness. When I think of peace, I think of the ocean; looking over the expanse of water is very calming to me. If I see the majestic waves that roll onto the beach and think of God's mighty power and all He can do in my life, then why, when it comes time to not worry, do I find myself falling back into that habit? When I hear about all the trials that Christians are going through, I have to ask myself, "How can one have true peace?"

How can we go to bed each night knowing that the Lord is working on our behalf? Psalm 4:8 says, "I will both lay me down in peace, and sleep: for thou, Lord, only makest me to dwell in safety." Here are a few thoughts that the Lord has shown me for how to have peace in my life. I know as I go throughout the day and remember these lessons, my day has a brighter outlook than when I think of all the things that the devil might throw in my path.

First of all, peace is learning to trust God in everything that happens. God is sovereign and knows what is best for each one of us, even though we might not think so. We need to remember that He sees the whole picture; we don't. My life verse is Romans 8:28; and it surely gives me comfort knowing that God is going to work all things out for good in my life.

Secondly, peace is praying and giving our burdens to God. Philippians 4:6-7 says, "Be careful for nothing; but in every thing by prayer and supplication with thanksgiving let your requests be made known unto God. And the peace of God, which passeth all understanding, shall keep your hearts and minds through Christ Jesus." A major part of having peace is thanking the Lord for all things, whether good or bad.

Thirdly, peace is knowing the Holy Spirit's presence is with us as we walk throughout the day. John 14:16 reminds us that the Comforter will abide with us forever. He is there to help us if only we would ask.

We can choose to have peace in our present circumstances or choose to not trust God and be anxious. You see, ladies, everything boils down to the choices that we make. Philippians 4:9 says, "Those things, which ye have both learned, and received, and heard, and seen in me, do: and the God of peace shall be with you." As my key verse says in Isaiah 26:3, it is all about keeping our minds on Jesus that will keep us in true, perfect peace. How do we keep our minds on Jesus? It is being in His presence daily through Bible reading, prayer, and having an intimate relationship with Him.

peace

Notes:

Prayer Requests:

Lay Me Down in Peace

By Debra Lynn Birner

If it be possible, as much as lieth in you, live peaceably with all men.

Romans 12:18

When I have conflict in my life, I have no peace. Even a small conflict, a small dispute, a snarky comment, murmuring, or grumbling – all of these things can destroy my peace. I should know – before I was saved, my life was filled with conflict. It never crossed my mind at that time to esteem others better than myself. Not only did all that conflict and disputing destroy my peace, but it also also destroyed the peace of anyone with whom I came into contact. There were many sleepless nights, nights of despair dealing with my sin, my selfishness, my way – anything but peace.

I live a different life now – a life of peace. When I find that my peace has been disrupted, I do what I can quickly to remedy the situation. Often I find that my peace can be restored by simply reevaluating a situation, offering an apology for any wrongdoing on my part, always offering forgiveness for any perceived wrongdoing on another's part, and asking God to help me have peace with both God and man. I want to live peaceably with all men.

Conflict inevitably arises as we all have to deal with each other – sinners dealing with sinners. However, I have made predetermined decisions that I will not let another's actions rob me of my peace – and I certainly am not going to just give away my peace anymore.

Maintaining peace does not mean that I refrain from speaking the truth, offering a rebuke when necessary, or taking a rebuke. Maintaining peace means that I try to handle situations the way I believe God would have me handle them, and then I leave the results up to God.

Galatiaans 2:20, "I am crucified with Christ: nevertheless I live; yet not I, but Christ liveth in me: and the life which I now live in the flesh I live by the faith of the Son of God, who loved me, and gave himself for me." I strive to not be offended – because it is not I that live. It's not about me. Giving my life to Christ, and all of my conflicts brings peace. Peace is so sweet.

Psalms 4:8, "I will both lay me down in peace, and sleep: for thou, Lord, only makest me dwell in safety."

peace

Notes:

Prayer Requests:

One Thing is Needful

By Sarah Russell

And Jesus answered and said unto her, Martha, Martha, thou art careful and troubled about many things: But one thing is needful: and Mary hath chosen that good part, which shall not be taken away from her.

Luke 10:41-42

CAREFUL - adj. Full of care; anxious; solicitous.
NEEDFUL - adj. Necessary, as supply or relief; requisite.
PEACEFUL - adj. Quiet; undisturbed; not in a state of war or commotion.

There's no joy or pride that comes with confessing that you struggle with anxiety, or as the Bible puts it "care" or "fretting." It can cause you to feel ashamed or embarrassed that you deal with anxiety. You are not alone. I'm with you, my friend. And God's Word has a good bit to say about it, as well as showing us that many people do struggle with cares and anxieties. But what should we do to conquer a mind full of care and anxieties? Let's look at a very "careful" woman in Luke 10.

I love this story about Mary, Martha, and Jesus. In this passage, Jesus is very clear and direct about Martha's anxieties and attitude in contrast to her sister. Mary chose the calm and restful place of peace at His feet.

I first noticed how Jesus says Martha is "careful." She is full of care (anxiety), and she is troubled about many things. She's trying to serve Jesus, the people in her home, and make sure there is plenty of food.

She feels she's doing it all herself, and she's stressed out. In her anxiety and stress, her immediate response is to be angry and to complain. And isn't that just how it is? When we allow our mind to become so full with worry, stress, and anxiety we respond, often quickly, in agitation or anger. You can be sure complaining will not be far behind. If not verbally, then in our mind which is really just complaining to the Lord? That is exactly what Martha did. She allowed the stress of her present circumstances to fill her with anxiety, which robbed her of the peace and joy of actually being with and serving Jesus. When we are anxious and agitated to the point of anger because of circumstances or other's actions, we are sinning, plain and simple.

So what could Martha have done about her careful and troubled mind? Martha should have chosen to sit at the Master's feet for a while quietly listening to His words and basking in His sweet presence, giving Him her troubled mind, focusing solely on Him. That is what we should choose to do as well. Being in His presence is that "one needful thing" that Jesus spoke about. The work can wait; the cooking can wait; life can wait. Take the time to sit at your Lord's feet. Open your Bible and hear what He has to say. Spend time in prayer. Start by thanking Him for being so good, worship your King, and count your many blessings. Peace and calm will come through the Word and time spent in quiet prayer and worship. Remember Isaiah 26:3, "Thou wilt keep him in perfect peace, whose mind is stayed on thee: because he trusteth in thee." Steady your mind on the Saviour and reflect on His sweet and precious promises. Choose the one thing that is needful, and you will be living a peaceful life rather than a careful life.

peace

Notes:

Prayer Requests:

Where to Find Peace

By Sharon Garrett

*For He is our peace, who hath made both one,
and hath broken down the middle wall of partition between us;*

Ephesians 2:14

We all know what it is to go through difficulties and times in life that disturb us and cause anguish and pain. As I was looking at the definition of the word *peace* it means "freedom from disturbance." I remembered those times when I was disturbed. What brought calm and peace to my heart? The Lord Jesus did. Whether it was just calling upon His Name or a longer time of prayer or a study of a particular passage of Scripture, that is where I found peace.

I reflected on the time before my salvation and how there was constant turmoil in my heart and soul. I remember the day that Colossians 1:20, "...having made peace through the blood...," became a reality in my life. When I called upon Him and He cleansed me with His blood, there was an unexplainable peace in my heart.

Then, I recalled times of trouble, serious illnesses, and danger on the mission field, and Ephesians 2:14 came to my mind, "For He is our peace." People would ask us – "How can you stay on the mission field in a country where terrorists reign and car bombs are exploding throughout the city where you live?" "He is our peace." He had led us there to labor for Him – He will fulfill His promise. "Peace I leave with you, my peace I give unto you..." John 14:27.

Today, in this world filled with turmoil, tragedy, and wickedness, again I turn to the verse we love so well, "Looking unto Jesus..." Hebrews 12:2a. Why? He is our peace.

Many hearts are filled with fear over the future of our own country because it has forsaken God and His commandments. But Galatians 3:15 says, "Let the peace of God rule in your hearts...." How precious to have peace in our hearts, peace with God, and the peace of God.

Do you have that peace in salvation? What about during difficulties, sickness, and trials? Jesus is our peace! Turn to Him and trust Him!

> When I called upon Him and He cleansed me with His blood, there was an unexplainable peace in my heart.

Peace in a Crazy World

By Kate Ledbetter

Behold, the hour cometh, yea, is now come, that ye shall be scattered, every man to his own, and shall leave me alone: and yet I am not alone, because the Father is with me. These things I have spoken unto you, that in me ye might have peace. In the world ye shall have tribulation: but be of good cheer; I have overcome the world.

John 16:32-33

There are times that I wonder how much worse it will get before the Lord returns. I see sin on every side, and the pull that the world has even on the church. Very often, I give into the sadness of it all, and I lose my focus on the truth. The truth is that Jesus said for His disciples to "be of good cheer." Why? Because He has "overcome the world."

Tribulation means "pressure; affliction; anguish; burden; persecution; trouble." Jesus was conveying to the disciples that peace could come in the midst of it all if they anchored themselves in Him. So often, when tribulation comes, I find myself trying to find understanding. In my flesh, I feel that if I can gain understanding, I will then find comfort and peace. That is such a false hope.

Peace can only be found in Christ alone. I have found that every time I give Him the situation and anchor in Him, He gives not only peace but also the understanding I was so desperately searching for, to begin with.

Peace simply means "quietness and rest." If you're searching for quietness and rest today in a tumultuous world, be of good cheer! Anchor in Christ and the reality that He has already overcome the world! We are living in defeated territory — the world just doesn't know it yet. Live victoriously today because you know the Victor! No matter what we face, He is a God of infinite understanding, and in that, we can rest! Be of good cheer!

> The truth is that Jesus said for His disciples to "be of good cheer."

Left with the "Peaces"

By Cherith Shiflett

Peace I leave with you, my peace I give unto you; not as the world giveth, give I unto you. Let not your heart be troubled, neither let it be afraid.

John 14:27

I recently heard a thought that really stuck with me. At the cross, Jesus left something for everyone. For his mother, he left a caretaker in John, the soldiers left with his gambled robe, and loyal Joseph of Arimathea was given his body to bury... but what did he leave behind for us?

Before his death Jesus said these words to his disciples " Peace I leave with you, my peace I give unto you; not as the world giveth, give I unto you. Let not your heart be troubled, neither let it be afraid." Even then, Jesus was reassuring them that he wasn't just going to go back to Heaven and forget about them. He left them with His peace. We get to claim that promise too!

The peace God gives is something this world will never understand.

1. **WE CAN HAVE PEACE IN OUR ETERNITY.**

Romans 5:1 says "Therefore being justified by faith, we have peace with God through our Lord Jesus Christ:" Because of Calvary, we don't have to worry or fret about where we will spend eternity. I can't imagine going through life not knowing what happens after death. I have a very curious nature and not knowing would have cost me many sleepless nihts. In fact, as a 7 year old girl, I was saved around 1 A.M. because I refused to sleep not knowing where I would spend eternity. I had to get that settled. We get to look forward to Heaven and seeing our Savior! What a relief to know I have a home in Heaven.

2. **WE CAN HAVE PEACE IN OUR ETHICS.**

Psalms 119:165 "Great peace have they which love thy law: and nothing shall offend them." I've always liked this verse. If you are easily offended, you're not reading your Bible enough. If you are easily offended, you think too highly of yourself. If you are easily offended, you're not living with the fruits of the Spirit. If you're easily offended, you're not living according to God's law. As Christians, we don't have the liberty to be easily offended. Thankfully, we don't have to live in a constant pity party. Get in God's Word, there is peace to be found in simply following his Word. Put others first - when you're thinking of others, you don't have time to worry about yourself.

3. WE CAN HAVE PEACE AT THE END.

Romans 12:18 "If it be possible, live peaceably with all men." For me, when I came to Christ, peace was one of the "tangible" things I felt. Instantaneous peace flooded my heart when I asked the Lord to save me. I feel that peace as I lay my head on the pillow at night. I feel that peace when I think about the unknown future. And one day, I know I'll feel that peace as I breathe my last breath.

I'm so thankful that God left us with His peace. It is real and undeniable. I've seen the evidences of peace in my life and in the lives of others. I've watched other Christians go through trials with a peace that is unexplainable. The peace God gives is something this world will never understand. They are searching in all the wrong places, trying to find rest in an exhausting world, trying to find quiet in the loudness. We have the answers they're looking for. Lord, help us to be willing to share you and the peace you gave us with others!

peace

Notes:

Prayer Requests:

Peace in Decision Making

By Hannah Kasprzyk

And let the peace of God rule in your hearts....

Colossians 3:15a

To be honest, I have the tendency to be an indecisive person. I have worked hard in recent years to be better at making decisions, but I still struggle. There have been moments in my life when I was nervous about what was going to happen and afraid that I would make the wrong choice. Why? I was missing God's peace. By definition, peace is a quietness of the mind, a calmness. Peace grows an assurance in the decision that no matter what the repercussions might be, it is still the right choice. Finding peace in the decision-making process can be a vital factor for a Christian. When I have peace in my heart, then I know things will turn out for my good and God's glory. How can I ensure that I have peace about making the right decision?

First of all, peace is found in God's Word. Psalm 119:165 says, "Great peace have they which love thy law: and nothing shall offend them." When your decision aligns with biblical principles, peace will follow. I challenge you to read and really meditate on Proverbs 3:1-17.

Peace can be added to your life when you keep God's commandments (v2). Finding wisdom not only brings happiness, but it also leads to peace (v13, 17).

Secondly, peace with making a decision can be acquired through godly counsel. God has purposely placed authorities in all of our lives to help guide us in our decisions. This could be your pastor and his wife, your parents, or other seasoned saints of God who have experience in that particular area. They want to be there to help you through those pivotal points in life; let them be a part of the process. Proverbs 11:14 states, "Where no counsel is, the peoplve fall: but in the multitude of counselors there is safety." There have been many times godly counsel has saved a person from making terrible decisions that would have hurt and even ruined his life. If you heed godly counsel, you will find peace in your decision.

Thirdly, being spiritually minded will bring peace even in making the hardest of decisions. Romans 8:6 says, "For to be carnally minded is death; but to be spiritually minded is life and peace." Are you following the leading of the Holy Spirit or are you convinced you know better? Remember the warning in Jeremiah 17:9, "The heart is deceitful above all things, and desperately wicked: who can know it?"

Is a decision staring you in the face? Are you looking for that quiet, calm assurance that you are making the right decision? Use God's formula for making decisions and sit back as God's peace floods over you.

peace

Notes:

Prayer Requests:

The Ornament of a Peaceful Spirit

By Susan Hutchens

But let it be the hidden man of the heart, in that which is not corruptible, even the ornament of a meek and quiet spirit, which is in the sight of God of great price.

I Peter 3:4

I have a friend who bought a collection of used Christmas ornaments when she and her husband were first married over thirty years ago. These ornaments weren't anything special, just old glass balls and garland that were a little worn out back then and probably pretty shabby by now. One day, I asked her if she still had those old ornaments after so many years. She immediately responded, "Yes! We bought those at the beginning of our marriage, and we have loved them so much through the years. They're precious to me!" Those ornaments are precious to her, although they might look like cheap baubles to someone else, and she values them enough to keep using them year after year. Their value is in the eye of their owner.

Similarly, God has an ornament that is precious in His eyes: a woman who has a "meek and quiet spirit." Many people consider meekness and quietness to be cheap baubles, qualities that render a woman less than worthy, weak, and timid. But God sees these character traits as being of great value! That quiet spirit is calm, undisturbed, peaceable, and free from alarm.

For most of us, a peaceful spirit does not come naturally. We look at the state of the world and our country, we look at our problems, we worry about our children, we fret over relationships, we stew over what might happen—there are troubles everywhere we look. Our spirits get "all ruffled up," as I describe it to my husband. But God desires for us to have a peaceful spirit in spite of all these things.

How can we develop a peaceful spirit in a world that is not peaceful at all? We can ask God for help. He loves to freely give us all things (Romans 8:32)! We can bring our thoughts into captivity to Christ (II Corinthians 10:5), thinking on the "good things" (Philippians 4:8). We can "study to be quiet"—work at being peaceful (I Thessalonians 4:11). We can also choose our companions carefully (I Corinthians 15:33). Ain't nobody got time for that gal that's constantly upset and trying to bring us along for the ride!

Just as we choose ornaments we consider beautiful, so God has chosen to adorn women with an ornament He considers beautiful: a quiet spirit. Let's work at having peaceful spirits! "To go on from one day to the next, leaving the unsettling things with God, being free and whole and serene because we are secure in our home—this is what 'dwelling' in Christ and His love means." – Elisabeth Elliot.

peace

Notes:

Prayer Requests:

Peace is the "Piece to the Puzzle"

By Catherine Aylor

And the peace of God which passeth all understanding, shall keep your hearts and mind through Christ Jesus.

Philippians 4:7

The Lord shall fight for you, and ye shall hold your peace.

Exodus 14:14

When I am writing a devotional or a lesson for when I speak at the ladies' homeless shelter I head up for our church, it's a great honor. I don't want to write something, add some verses, and call it a day. I pray; I seek; I ask. I want to know that God is in my words because they should be His not mine. There I was writing on the topic of "peace," yet I couldn't get peace about what to write. I didn't know what was waiting just a few weeks away that was going to require God's peace that passes all understanding.

This week we faced a great tragedy. We have dealt with some things no one should ever have to go through. Although those around us loved and cared for us, there was not too much they could do or say that would help. It was really a battle the Lord needed to fight. When I realized I felt overwhelmed by the circumstances we were, and are, and

Let go of the piece you are staring at and grab hold of His peace!

will face, it was unbearable. It was causing great stress, but then the Lord reminded me of a lesson I taught many years ago.

I remember getting a calendar with those really pretty butterflies on the monthly pictures. Each of those butterflies was beautiful in the full picture, but what I did is I put that paper picture on a piece of cardboard and then cut it up into forty different pieces. I then numbered the backs of each one to know which piece would go where later. I took a piece in my hand. It was a part of the wing. I knew because I had seen the picture before I cut it up. Looking at it, it was just shaded black with white spots and unless someone had seen the full picture, the piece was unknown.

I remember speaking and handing out a piece to each lady. I asked them to tell me what piece they were holding. No one could tell me. I had a board in the front. As I taught, I asked for the pieces in numeric order, and I put them on the board. After the first rowf, you could start to see, and with each piece being placed, it was clearer and clearer.

You see, when we are facing a battle, tragedy, or a great trial, we are looking to take care of it. The problem is we are staring at the small piece of the puzzle and have no idea where the piece fits. That piece belongs to God. God is on your side. Never let the piece of the puzzle of your life you are facing cause you to dwell too much in or on your circumstances. It will keep you from having the "peace" of understanding the Lord gives. No matter what you are going through, God's got it. Let go of the piece you are staring at and grab hold of His peace! Each puzzle piece in life is and will be made clearer each day and ultimately in the end. God knows the end from the beginning. Let Him lead the way with the comfort that He provides. Because when you allow the peace that passes all understanding to rule in your heart, no "piece" of life will ever be unclear again!

The Master's Puzzle

The puzzle piece did not fit where it was placed.
I tried to find another spot, but there was no available space.
I began to look at the piece and figure out what it might be.
I kept looking and wondering where it might go, but I could not see.

"This piece could not belong to this puzzle," I thought to myself today.
Then I realized I was looking at it in a very wrong way.
It was turned upside down and needed to be flipped around.
Realizing this was the problem, then the placement was quickly found.

It did not take me long to realize the perspective was all wrong.
I was dwelling on the place where I thought it might belong.
Many times, we do the same thing in life and think we know best.
When to sit, where to stand, or the answers to the test.

We might think that we know what God has in His will for us.
We then become prideful and forget in Him we are to trust.
We are trying to go anyplace we think we might fit in today.
But where we are supposed to be could not be found that way.

We forgot to ask our Father to show us the way He wants us to go.
We thought we were doing His will, but little did we know.
Where we thought we belonged was just a trap, you see.
We were not mindful of the place He needed us to be.

Sometimes in this puzzle of life, the answers are not always clear.
The only way to know sometimes is to stand still, listen, and hear.
It may not be easy to do, and you may think there is a better way.
But hold on He may flip your world upside down; just say:

"Thank you, Lord, for making this piece fit where you want it to.
Thank you for helping me see I can do all things through You!"
All the pieces fit in the big picture we do not get to see,
But it will be a Masterpiece when He is finished with you and me.

What the Lost are Looking For: Peace

By Hannah Suttle

Thou wilt keep him in perfect peace whose mind is stayed on thee: because he trusteth in thee.

Isaiah 26:3

Peace is what people are seeking. Peace is what the world wants. We, as Christians, know that peace comes through Christ, and when we try to do things our own way in our own time, there is no peace in our heart. The peace in our relationship with God carries over to our relationships with others in our lives as well. Can anyone else testify to the fact that your day is a bit more stressful and people are just a bit more annoying when you neglect to have your personal time with the Lord in the morning? The flesh will always be an enemy to peace. If our mind is stayed upon God's Word and rests on the Lord, then we will find peace in our hearts and lives.

I recently heard of a pastor's testimony that I'd like to share with you. This man had been raised Catholic and knew about God without ever truly knowing Him personally. He had heard people talk about hell and had been in and out of church, but religion was just "not his thing." He tried everything the world had to offer and was not completely unsatisfied, but still felt as if he were missing just one thing – peace.

While walking down the street after leaving a bar, he ran across a street preacher who asked him a simple question: "Sir, do you have peace in your heart?" This caught him off guard. As a matter of fact, nothing he'd ever had or tried brought him peace. The preacher continued to say, "I can show you how you can have peace." He then, of course, continued to share the gospel and how Jesus had given him peace when he was born again. The man was then saved, continued to grow, and now is the pastor of a great church. And all of this came from? A simple answer to someone looking for peace: Jesus.

This came as an amazing challenge to me in soulwinning. I started asking a few people at different doors if they had peace or knew how they could get to a place in their life where they had it. The response honestly surprised me. People are so eager to hear about how they can find peace! So I'll end with a challenge to you that I've taken myself: ask a few people you know if they have peace. It is such an amazing way to open up a conversation about the gospel. Once you are able to share with people how they can be saved, they too can find peace with God by trusting in Him.

Peace...Even There

By Kelly Byrley

Whither shall I go from thy spirit? or whither shall I flee from thy presence? If I ascend up into heaven, thou art there: if I make my bed in hell, behold, thou art there. If I take the wings of the morning, and dwell in the uttermost parts of the sea; Even there shall thy hand lead me, and thy right hand shall hold me.

Psalm 139:7-10

The words "even there" in the above passage have brought me comfort so many times. It has reminded me that no matter where I am, the Lord is with me. I have had some fantastic,

joyous, and abundant "even there" times. I have also had many comfortable and average "even there" times. And then there are the other "even there" times. The ones we do not enjoy. The "even there" times where trials come in like tsunamis bringing emergencies, frightening events, and soul-crushing heartbreaks. Often those times are fleeting and pass fairly quickly, but sometimes we must endure them for a longer season. I can remember two very long seasons when I faced so many struggles back-to-back that they shook me to my core and threatened to take me out. But God! (I love saying that. It's so powerful and it's so true!)

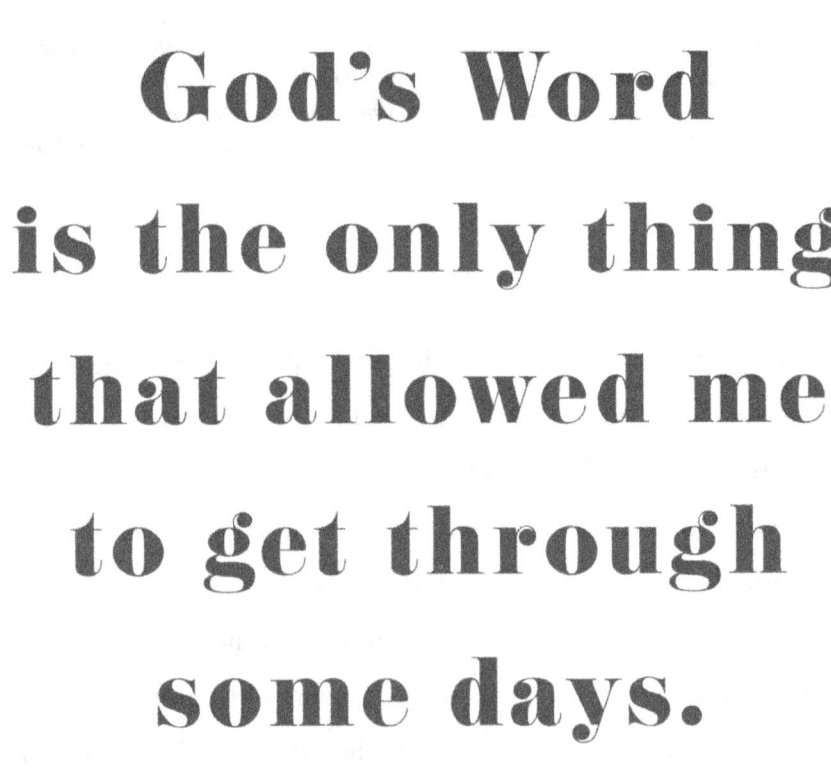

God's Word is the only thing that allowed me to get through some days.

During one of those seasons, in particular, I struggled mentally and physically. I knew I couldn't also struggle spiritually, or I would be a goner. There were two different times when I was so mentally overwhelmed that I couldn't remember how to get home, and I suffered from panic attacks for a short while. Just having my Bible with me gave me comfort. So I pretty much took It everywhere I went. I wore that Bible out! There were times that I laid It next to me with my hand on It as I slept because It was the only way I could truly rest. Other times, I would ask the Lord to give me something that I needed and as I opened my Bible, my eyes would land on a verse that was perfect for what I was dealing with.

I cannot explain it to you, but when I read my Bible, especially in Psalms, it was like I could feel the Word of God pour over my soul and seep in, soothing the broken areas and literally refreshing my spirit. It was like a breath of air into struggling lungs. For years, I had made a habit of writing Bible verses on index cards cut in half and hole-punched on a book ring. I took that ring almost everywhere as well. I meditated on verses like Isaiah 43:2, Philippians 4:7, Psalm 4:8, Psalm 147:3, Proverbs 21:31, Psalm 46, Psalm 61, and countless others, including the passage I quoted earlier from Psalm 139. Those passages reminded me of God's love for me and that God was aware of what I was going through and that He was with me, "even there." God's Word is the only Thing that allowed me to get through some days.

If you are going through a difficult season, don't give up! Staying the course is always worth it! Keep your Bible close. Meditate on It. Allow It to speak peace to your soul. Beg the Lord for help.

He will respond! As I look back now on those difficult times, I am so grateful that I was able to cling to the Lord and that He clung to me when I was too weak to hang on myself. None of us like to go through difficulties, but sometimes they are necessary so we learn how to allow the Lord to comfort us and then in turn, we can comfort others.

II Corinthians 1:3-4 says, "Blessed be God, even the Father of our Lord Jesus Christ, the Father of mercies, and the God of all comfort; Who comforteth us in all our tribulation, that we may be able to comfort them which are in any trouble, by the comfort wherewith we ourselves are comforted of God." There is no greater comfort than the Word of God.

The phrase "even there" in Psalm 139:10 is a constant reminder that no matter where we are, we are never alone and we are never lost. Whether it's rejoicing in gladness at the top of a victorious mountain, resting peacefully by the still waters, hobbling along the rough terrain of a valley, scared and hiding in the shadows of darkness, seeking refuge when we are wounded and broken, climbing boldly to the Rock that is higher than us, or anywhere in between ... that, my friend, is "even there."

peace

Notes:

Prayer Requests:

About The Authors

Each author has been handpicked because of their Christian testimony. God has gifted each writer with incredibly versatile perspectives of the Christian life. These godly ladies come from all walks of life including pastor's wives and daughters, missionary wives, church staff ladies, and faithful church members. Their written words of wisdom are sure to bless your heart.

To know more about our writers please visit:
thehighlyfavouredlife.com/our-story

Salvation Made Simple
By Renee Patton

Admit. One must first admit they are a sinner. Romans 3:10 states, "As it is written, There is none righteous, no, not one." Sin is everywhere and we all commit sin, many times without even trying. Perhaps in a conversation, we say something innocently, then realize it was not correct. That, my friend, is lying. Of course, murder is a sin that is seen and felt by those affected. However, lying is too. Jeremiah reminds one that "The heart is deceitful above all things, and desperately wicked: who can know it?" (17:9). A baby does not have to be told how to sin, it is simply in our nature. One must admit they are a sinner otherwise we make God a liar as found in I John 1:10, "If we say that we have not sinned, we make him a liar, and his word is not in us."

Believe. One must believe Jesus came to this earth to be born and die for our sins. "For God so loved the world, that he gave his only begotten Son, that whosoever believeth in him should not peish, but have everlasting life" (John 3:16). God desires that we should not perish, thus the choice is ours. God gives man the opportunity for salvation if man would take it. Romans 5:8 states "But God commendeth his love toward us, in that, while we were yet sinners, Christ died for us." Webster's 1828 Dictionary defines commendeth as entrusts or gives. So, God gave us His love through His Son, Jesus. Furthermore, Romans 5:19 shows how sin came from Adam and is made righteous through Christ, "For as by one man's disobedience [Adam] many were made sinners [mankind], so by the obedience of one [Jesus] shall many [mankind] be made righteous."

Confess. Confession is made with one's own mouth. The words must come from the person alone. Romans 10:9 talks of both confession and believing, "That if thou shalt confess with thy mouth the lord Jesus, and shalt believe in thine heart that God hath raised him from the dead, thou shalt be saved." The key is I have to confess to God. My husband or friend cannot confess for me. While God gives man the opportunity on earth, there will be a time every knee will bow and confess God is Lord, "For it is written, As I live, saith the Lord, every knee shall bow to me, and every tongue shall confess to God" (Romans 14:11).

To see more resources on salvation visit:
https://www.thehighlyfavouredlife.com/simple-salvation

If you made this decision, please contact us at *highlyfavouredlife @gmail.com*. We would love to rejoice with you in the new life you now have in Christ.

www.ingramcontent.com/pod-product-compliance
Lightning Source LLC
Chambersburg PA
CBHW060324050426
42449CB00011B/2633